Joyful Creation Series
So Great a Love

Written and illustrated by
Kristie Wilde

Published by Wilde Art Press
10 9 8 7 6 5 4 3 2

Copyright © 2017, Kristie Wilde
Written and Illustrated by Kristie Wilde

All rights reserved

ISBN-13: 978-0-9974828-1-2
ISBN-10: 0-9974828-1-2

To my children and my children's children, and to all children everywhere.
May you know the God of creation and the great love He has for you!

Thank you to my Lord Jesus Christ and to you, Mom, for your continuous support and encouragement.

Higher than the mountains and wider than the desert . . .

so great is God's love for you!

He wants to gather you . . .

. . . as a hen gathers her chicks.

. . . just like a mama bear protects her cubs!

God's love will help you . . .

. . . like a koala helps her young.

. . . as the bird hides her babies!

God will clean your heart with His great love . . .

. . . as the lioness washes her cub.

. . . as the shepherd watches over his flocks.

His love is refreshing . . .

. . . like an oasis in the desert for the camels.

. . . like water delights the otters!

. . . He will always love you!

Scriptures

"Your unfailing love, O LORD, is as vast as the heavens; Your faithfulness reaches beyond the clouds." Psalm 36:5, NLT

"How often I wanted to gather your children together, the way a hen gathers her chicks under her wings..." Mat.23:37, NAS

"But let all those who take refuge in You rejoice - let them always shout for joy, because You defend them. Let them also who love Your name be joyful in You." Psalm 5:11, NHEB

"Praise the Lord, day by day. God our Savior helps us." Psalm 68:19, ICB

"For He will conceal me there when troubles come. He will hide me in His sanctuary. He will place me out of reach on a high rock." Psalm 27:5, NLT

"If we confess our sins, He is faithful and just to forgive us our sins, and to cleanse us from all unrighteousness." 1 John 1:19, KJV

"He tends His flock like a shepherd. He gathers the lambs in His arms and carries them close to His heart. He gently leads those that have young." Isaiah 40:11, NIV

"I will give rest and strength to those who are weak and tired." Jeremiah 31:25, ICB

". . . He will take delight in you with gladness. With his love, he will calm all your fears. He will rejoice over you with joyful songs."" Zephaniah 3:17, NLT

Jesus said, "Let the little children come to Me, and do not hinder them, for the kingdom of heaven belongs to such as these." Luke 18:16, NIV

Author and Illustrator, Kristie Wilde

As a mother and Grandmother, Kristie Wilde enjoys going on adventures with children. She loves to see their eyes light up as they discover some new, exciting treasure – especially when that treasure is a nugget of insight about God and His creation. Because books are such a wonderful way to go exploring, Kristie has been inspired to utilize her experience with nature, together with her love for Jesus and her artistic gift, to create beautiful, insightful children's books that light up the eyes of their readers - launching the *Joyful Creation* series.

She has authored, illustrated, and published two books in this series: the first book, *Made for a Purpose,* and this book, *So Great a Love,* is the second.

She has illustrated and published Judy Watson's delightful children's books, *Shooting Stars and Satellites, Green Smoothies and Brain Talk, All About Me* and *In My World.*

As the owner and artistic source of Wilde Art, and Wilde Art Press in Sonora, California, Kristie manages her projects from concept to completion. She enlivens them with watercolor illustrations in a realistic style, adding whimsical touches.

She blends her talents as an artist and illustrator, her expertise in Photoshop, and her experience communicating educational concepts - gained while working with the Interpretive Department of the U.S. Forest Service - to create beautiful, detailed, and insightful illustrations.

Kristie has a degree in Forestry, which gives her an excellent knowledge base from which to pull accurate educational information.

The U.S. Forest Service and the Tri-Dam Project have commissioned Kristie to illustrate interpretive signage for them along the Highway 108 corridor through the Sierra Nevada mountains.

More works by Kristie can be seen on her websites: wilde-art.com and wildeartpress.com, and she can be contacted by email at kristie@wilde-art.com.

www.ingramcontent.com/pod-product-compliance
Lightning Source LLC
Chambersburg PA
CBHW041126300426
44113CB00002B/81